Printed in the USA

Printing by Tarco Press

Bindery by Lake Book Manufacturing

Design by ZGraphics, Ltd. • www.zgraphics.com

Zak & Lizzie

By Ann Malokas • Illustrated by Corasue Nicholas

Judy, with love laughs
and great memories...

Ann Malokas

To Zachary
With all our love
We see the world through your eyes

and for this we are truly blessed

This is the story of Zachary,
called Zak, nearly new
miniature human
and me, Lizzie,
his best friend,
shag mop dog.

I know something about
navigating among people
who are bigger and
move differently.

We're a dandy duo.

Who loves Zak?

Dad
Mom
Gramma and Grampa
Cousin Alexis
Gazillions of friends and family

And me, Lizzie, his best friend, shag mop dog. I lick his face and make him giggle. Be happy, Zak.

You are adored.

What makes Zak's day bright?

Sun on his face

Moon guarding his night

Gazillions of friends and family

Cousin Alexis

Gramma and Grampa

Mom

Dad

And me, Lizzie, his best
friend, shag mop dog. I am
a very patient wooly snuggly
just perfect for cuddling.
Rest easily, Zak.
You have grown today.

What are Zak's treasures?

Grass tickling his knees
Sand running through his fingers
Sun on his face
Moon guarding his night

Gazillions of friends and family
Cousin Alexis
Gramma and Grampa
Mom
Dad

And me, Lizzie, his best friend, shag mop dog. I nudge him to roll over. Use your hope, Zak, where your muscles are still new and challenged.

What are Zak's dreams?

Music of the breeze

Dandelion wings brushing his nose

Grass tickling his knees

Sand running through his fingers

Sun on his face

Moon guarding his night

Gazillions of friends and family
Cousin Alexis
Gramma and Grampa
Mom
Dad

And me, Lizzie, his best friend,
shag mop dog. I am most excellent
shaman for the boy who sees with
his soul what others can't see with
their eyes.

Tell us the secrets, Zak!

What are Zak's special needs?

Gingerbread sniffs
Stars twinkling
Music of the breeze
Dandelion wings brushing his nose
Grass tickling his knees
Sand running through his fingers
Sun on his face
Moon guarding his night

Gazillions of friends and family
Cousin Alexis
Gramma and Grampa
Mom
Dad

And me, Lizzie, his best friend, shag
mop dog. I know when to lie quietly
and when to leap with joy.
Dance with your heart, Zak.

What are things
that help Zak grow?

Ladybug luck
Rhythm of the gardens
Gingerbread sniffs
Stars twinkling
Music of the breeze
Dandelion wings brushing his nose
Grass tickling his knees
Sand running through his fingers
Sun on his face
Moon guarding his night

Gazillions of friends and family
Cousin Alexis
Gramma and Grampa
Mom
Dad

And me, Lizzie, his best friend,
shag mop dog. I make him feel
safe when the village seems
new and scary.

Know I will be
here for you, Zak.

What does Zak find
in our big world?

Smooth rocks

Water falls

Ladybug luck

Rhythm of the gardens

Gingerbread sniffs

Stars twinkling

Music of the breeze

Dandelion wings brushing his nose

Grass tickling his knees

Sand running through his fingers

Sun on his face

Moon guarding his night

Gazillions of friends and family

Cousin Alexis

Gramma and Grampa

Mom

Dad

And me, Lizzie, his best friend,
shag mop dog. I watch others
whisper and shake their heads
about this angel child just because
his eyes are without sight and his
limbs must work with extra burdens.
Use your wings, Zak.
Horizons call you.

Wherever Zak goes,
I will be, me Lizzie,
his best friend,
shag mop dog.

I know something about navigating
among people
who are bigger
and move differently.

We're a dandy duo.

Zak & Lizzie is a heart-warming and true story of a visually impaired boy named Zak and his friend Lizzie, a "shag-mop" dog. The story of Zak & Lizzie tells of Zak's friendship with Lizzie. In the story, Lizzie helps Zak to see and Zak teaches others to see not only with their eyes, but with their hearts and souls.

Zak & Lizzie is beautifully written and illustrated. This special book for children and adults of all ages was created for Zachary and the One Small Voice Foundation. The One Small Voice Foundation was created to raise money for the research of optic nerve hypoplasia.

Zachary was born with optic nerve hypoplasia, which is the absence or underdevelopment of the optic nerve. It is the leading cause of blindness in children in the United States. The monies generated by the sale of this book will go towards the research of optic nerve hypoplasia. We hope that research will one day lead to a cure and prevention of this eye disease.

Thank you for supporting our cause and we hope you enjoy this beautiful story as much as we do!

For more information on optic nerve hypoplasia, visit our website at www.onesmallvoicefoundation.org

About the Author

Ann Malokas is married and mother to three grown children, two sons and one daughter. When her children were too old to need her, she found children to love and fill the empty nest as a childcare worker. She is also a professional clown and storyteller, sometimes dressed as Mother Goose or Ms. Santa Claus. She has published a book for moms called *"Love, Ms. Santa."* Most of her writing is for, and about, children.

About the Artist

Corasue Nicholas is a freelance book
designer and children's textbook
illustrator based in northwest Indiana.
Other children's books she has
illustrated include *Women Scientists
and Inventors* and *Ancient Egyptians
and Their Neighbors*. Corasue also
paints in acrylics, and recently was
commissioned to create a wall-sized
mural for a children's activity room
at a nature center.